FRANCIS FRITH'S
DUDLEY LIVING MEMORIES

HAPPY RETIREMENT MARTIN

HOPE YOU ENJOY THE WALK DOWN MEMORY LANE

CHRIS

THE FRANCIS FRITH COLLECTION

www.francisfrith.com

FRANCIS FRITH'S

DUDLEY

LIVING MEMORIES

PAUL COLLINS is a historian, writer and broadcaster, specialising in the history of transport and of his native Black Country. Born in Wolverhampton, Paul has lived in Wollaston, Stourbridge all his life. After many years spent as a student, researcher and lecturer at Birmingham University, Paul now works part-time as a conservation officer as well as running his own consultancy as a historic buildings analyst. A prolific author, Paul has published 16 books and numerous articles, and is a frequent speaker and lecturer. Broadcasting is another of Paul's interests, and in addition to trying to launch a radio station in Stourbridge, he is also a regular broadcaster on radio and on television, including work for the Open University. He also supplies archive film to television companies from his own collection.

DUDLEY
LIVING MEMORIES

DR PAUL COLLINS

First published in the United Kingdom in 2005
by The Francis Frith Collection

Limited Hardback Edition 2005 ISBN 1-84589-047-7

Paperback Edition 2005 ISBN 1-85937-972-9

British Library Cataloguing in Publication Data

Dudley - Living Memories
Dr Paul Collins

The Francis Frith Collection
Frith's Barn, Teffont,
Salisbury, Wiltshire SP3 5QP
Tel: +44 (0) 1722 716 376
Email: info@francisfrith.co.uk
www.francisfrith.co.uk

Printed and bound in Great Britain

Front Cover: Dudley, *The Castle Keep c1955* D103019t
Frontispiece: Dudley, *The View from the Castle Keep c1955* D103054

The colour-tinting is for illustrative purposes only, and is not intended to be historically accurate

Aerial photographs reproduced under licence from
Simmons Aerofilms Limited.
Historical Ordnance Survey maps reproduced under licence from Homecheck.
co.uk

Every attempt has been made to contact copyright holders of
illustrative material. We will be happy to give full acknowledgement in future
editions for any items not credited. Any information should be directed to The
Francis Frith Collection.

AS WITH ANY HISTORICAL DATABASE THE FRITH ARCHIVE IS CONSTANTLY
BEING CORRECTED AND IMPROVED AND THE PUBLISHERS WOULD WELCOME
INFORMATION ON OMISSIONS
OR INACCURACIES

CONTENTS

FRANCIS FRITH
VICTORIAN PIONEER

FRANCIS FRITH, founder of the world-famous photographic archive, was a complex and multi-talented man. A devout Quaker and a highly successful Victorian businessman, he was philosophical by nature and pioneering in outlook.

By 1855 he had already established a wholesale grocery business in Liverpool, and sold it for the astonishing sum of £200,000, which is the equivalent today of over £15,000,000. Now a very rich man, he was able to indulge his passion for travel. As a child he had pored over travel books written by early explorers, and his fancy and imagination had been stirred by family holidays to the sublime mountain regions of Wales and Scotland. 'What lands of spirit-stirring and enriching scenes and places!' he had written. He was to return to these scenes of grandeur in later years to 'recapture the thousands of vivid and tender memories', but with a different purpose. Now in his thirties, and captivated by the new science of photography, Frith set out on a series of pioneering journeys up the Nile and to the Near East that occupied him from 1856 unti 1860.

INTRIGUE AND EXPLORATION

These far-flung journeys were packed with intrigue and adventure. In his life story, written when he was sixty-three, Frith tells of being held captive by bandits, and of fighting 'an awful midnight battle to the very point of surrender with a deadly pack of hungry, wild dogs'. Wearing flowing Arab costume, Frith arrived at Akaba by camel sixty years before Lawrence of Arabia, where he encountered 'desert princes and rival sheikhs, blazing with jewel-hilted swords'.

He was the first photographer to venture beyond the sixth cataract of the Nile. Africa was still the mysterious 'Dark Continent', and Stanley and Livingstone's historic meeting was a decade into the future. The conditions for picture taking confound belief. He laboured for hours in his wicker dark-room in the sweltering heat of the desert, while the volatile chemicals fizzed dangerously in their trays. Back in London he exhibited his photographs and was 'rapturously cheered' by members of the Royal Society. His reputation as a photographer was made overnight.

VENTURE OF A LIFE-TIME

Characteristically, Frith quickly spotted the opportunity to create a new business as a specialist publisher of photographs. He lived in an era of immense and sometimes violent change. For the poor in the early part of Victoria's reign work was exhausting and the hours long, and people had precious little free time to enjoy themselves. Most people had no transport other than a cart or gig at their disposal, and rarely

travelled far beyond the boundaries of their own town or village. However, by the 1870s the railways had threaded their way across the country, and Bank Holidays and half-day Saturdays had been made obligatory by Act of Parliament. All of a sudden the working man and his family were able to enjoy days out and see a little more of the world.

With typical business acumen, Francis Frith foresaw that these new tourists would enjoy having souvenirs to commemorate their days out. In 1860 he married Mary Ann Rosling and set out on a new career: his aim was to photograph every city, town and village in Britain. For the next thirty years he travelled the country by train and by pony and trap, producing fine photographs of seaside resorts and beauty spots that were keenly bought by millions of Victorians. These prints were painstakingly pasted into family albums and pored over during the dark nights of winter, rekindling precious memories of summer excursions.

THE RISE OF FRITH & CO

Frith's studio was soon supplying retail shops all over the country. To meet the demand he gathered about him a small team of photographers, and published the work of independent artist-photographers of the calibre of Roger Fenton and Francis Bedford. In order to gain some understanding of the scale of

Frith's business one only has to look at the catalogue issued by Frith & Co in 1886: it runs to some 670 pages, listing not only many thousands of views of the British Isles but also many photographs of most European countries, and China, Japan, the USA and Canada - note the sample page shown on page 9 from the hand-written Frith & Co ledgers recording the pictures. By 1890 Frith had created the greatest specialist photographic publishing company in the world, with over 2,000 sales outlets - more than the combined number that Boots and WH Smith have today! The picture on the next page shows the Frith & Co display board at Ingleton in the Yorkshire Dales (left of window). Beautifully constructed with a mahogany frame and gilt inserts, it could display up to a dozen local scenes.

POSTCARD BONANZA

The ever-popular holiday postcard we know today took many years to develop. In 1870 the Post Office issued the first plain cards, with a pre-printed stamp on one face. In 1894 they allowed other publishers' cards to be sent through the mail with an attached adhesive halfpenny stamp. Demand grew rapidly, and in 1895 a new size of postcard was permitted called the court card, but there was little room for illustration. In 1899, a year after Frith's death, a new card measuring 5.5 x 3.5 inches became the standard format, but it was not until 1902 that the divided back came into being, so that the address and message could be on one face and a full-size illustration on the other. Frith & Co were in the vanguard of postcard development: Frith's sons Eustace and Cyril continued their father's monumental task, expanding the number of views offered to the public and recording more and more places in Britain, as the coasts and countryside were opened up to mass travel.

Francis Frith had died in 1898 at his villa in Cannes, his great project still growing. The archive he created continued in business for another seventy years. By 1970 it contained over a third of a million pictures showing 7,000 British towns and villages.

FRANCIS FRITH'S LEGACY

Frith's legacy to us today is of immense significance and value, for the magnificent archive of evocative photographs he created provides a unique record of change in the cities, towns and villages throughout Britain over a century and more. Frith and his fellow studio photographers revisited locations many times down the years to update their views, compiling for us an enthralling and colourful pageant of British life and character.

We are fortunate that Frith was dedicated to recording the minutiae of everyday life, for it is this sheer wealth of visual data, the painstaking chronicle of changes in dress, transport, street layouts, buildings, housing, engineering and landscape that captivates us so much today. His remarkable images offer us a powerful link with the past and with the lives of our ancestors.

THE VALUE OF THE ARCHIVE TODAY

Computers have now made it possible for Frith's many thousands of images to be accessed almost instantly. Frith's images are increasingly used as visual resources, by social historians, by researchers into genealogy and ancestry, by architects and town planners, and by teachers involved in local history projects.

In addition, the archive offers every one of us an opportunity to examine the places where we and our families have lived and worked down the years. Highly successful in Frith's own era, the archive is now, a century and more on, entering a new phase of popularity. Historians consider the Francis Frith Collection to be of prime national importance. It is the only archive of its kind remaining in private ownership. Francis Frith's archive is now housed in an historic timber barn in the beautiful village of Teffont in Wiltshire. Its founder would not recognize the archive office as it is today. In place of the many thousands of dusty boxes containing glass plate negatives and an all-pervading odour of photographic chemicals, there are now ranks of computer screens. He would be amazed to watch his images travelling round the world at unimaginable speeds through internet lines.

The archive's future is both bright and exciting. Francis Frith, with his unshakeable belief in making photographs available to the greatest number of people, would undoubtedly approve of what is being done today with his lifetime's work. His photographs depicting our shared past are now bringing pleasure and enlightenment to millions around the world a century and more after his death.

DUDLEY
AN INTRODUCTION

Dudley's Origins and Early History

Dudley's name is derived from a personal name, Dudda, and the Old English term for a clearing or meadow, 'leah'; hence 'Dudda's Leah'. Anglo-Saxon charters of 779 give details of lands granted to Dudda, a minister of the Mercian King Offa. Other references include one to a Saxon prince Dudo in 760, who is said to have built a castle in the area, and another, in 836, to a Duda, an ealdorman, a chief or nobleman of the highest rank. Given the date range of these references it is unlikely that they all refer to the same person. Over time the name of Dudda's Leah was corrupted: Duddleye (1275), Doddeley (1279), Doddele (1330), Duddelegh (1360).

Geologically, the town stands on the ridge of the Pennine Chain; a line running from the top of Cawney Hill, along Hall Street, up the High Street to the parish church, and from there along Stafford Street and the Wolverhampton road, lies along the crest of this ridge. Water lying to the east of the ridge drains into the River Teme, which joins the Trent and ultimately the North Sea; water lying to the west of the ridge is absorbed by the River Stour, which joins the Severn and discharges into St George's Channel. To the north of the town

is Castle Hill, composed of Wenlock limestone of the Silurian system of Murchison, which has been extensively quarried.

Dudley was recorded thus in Domesday: 'The said William held Dudley; and there is his Castle'. It was a manorial borough by the 13th century, sending two members to the parliament of 1295. This status was uncommon at the time, and may have originated in a charter of 4 November 1218, which conferred rights and privileges upon the 'Burgesses of ye Borrow of Dudley'; much prosperity flowed as a result of the charter right giving exemption from tolls on things bought and sold. This empowered the burgesses to hold a market in which they could trade freely without paying the tolls outsiders were subject to.

Industrial Development

Exploitation of Dudley's natural resources began well before the Industrial Revolution, including both lime working and mining. The development of industry in Dudley followed the pattern of distribution of its natural resources, with which the area abounded. A 'pool' of coal and associated fireclay and ironstone surrounded the town centre, and the exploitation of these dictated the patterns of settlement and the subsequent development of the area. Lacking exploitable natural resources, the town centre became the site of many industries, most of which were in the Black Country tradition of 'metal bashing'.

By the mid 19th century a diverse series of industries had developed in Dudley, the most popular being maltsters, although they were on the decline. Fender and fire iron making, something of a Dudley specialty, was joined at a latter date by a related trade, bedstead making; and there was also nail making and dealing, which supported several other trades, such as cooperage and bag and twine making. The 20th century saw many of these industries contract in scale or disappear from the town altogether, a notable exception being the fender/fire iron/bedstead trade. Lost industries were replaced by newer ones, which reflected general industrial advances in the West Midlands. Thus a number of specialist engineering firms became established in Dudley, including those making cars and motor components. These firms were able to capitalise upon land reclaimed from former extractive industries and upon productive capacity built to meet the armament needs of the First World War. More recent years have seen a steady diminution in the town's traditional manufactures, notably that of fender and fire iron manufacture, and a rise in both light and heavy engineering. This was maintained through to the early 1970s, when the trend was first halted and then reversed following the general economic difficulties of the region and nation.

Transport

Lacking any naturally occurring waterways, and being such a locally important market town of long standing, Dudley gained and held on to this pre-eminence by virtue of its road communications. The 'Pennine Chain crest' route, from Rowley and through the town (Hall Street - High Street - Stafford Street - Wolverhampton Road), was an important packhorse route. During

The Castle Keep c1955 D103019

the 18th century several roads serving Dudley were turnpiked:

1727 - Great Bridge, via Dudley Port, through the town centre (Trindle Road-King Street) to Scott's Green (now the A461)
1727 - Halesowen through Old Hill and Netherton (now the A459)
1762 - Pedmore to Dudley (now the A4036 through Lye)
1762 - Blackheath via Rowley Regis (now the B4171)
1790 - Pattingham-Himley and Eve Hill (now the B4176)

Dudley's basic road network remained unchanged until the building of the Birmingham New Road. This was proposed as early as 1908, but was not fully surveyed until 1922. Construction began in 1924 and was facilitated by government funding to provide unemployment relief. The Prince of Wales officially opened the 9¾-mile road on 2 November 1927. Further road improvements were made piecemeal until the 1960s, when the town centre redevelopment of 1962-69 embraced the widening of King Street and the creation of the Flood Street car parks. Still greater changes came with the construction of the Dudley Southern By-Pass in the late 1990s.

The topography of Dudley town centre precluded its penetration by much of the Black Country canal network. A portion of the Birmingham Canal clips its corner. This was authorised on 24 February 1768 and came into use in May 1770. The Dudley and the Stourbridge canal schemes, south of the town centre, were proposed c1774, and a tunnel under the town linking them with the Birmingham line was constructed, at a cost of £50,000, over the next seven years. At 3,172 yards it was the fifth longest canal tunnel in the England. Its opening was announced on 15 October 1792. Commercial traffic ceased using it in 1951, but it stayed open for recreational use until 1982, when it closed owing to the poor condition of its brickwork. After lengthy repairs the tunnel opened on 21 June 1992 and was officially reopened on 3 September 1992. Lord Dudley & Ward's branch canal was begun c1775 to link the Birmingham line at Tipton with the Earl's lime workings at Castle Mill, where a basin was completed c1779; this now forms part of the Black Country Living Museum site. A later earl also built the Pensnett Canal in the late 1830s. This had no locks and ran for 1¼ miles from a basin at The Wallows to join the Dudley Canal near Dudley Tunnel. It opened in 1840.

Dudley was once well served by railways, having the lines of two different companies meeting at a joint station at the foot of Castle Hill. The first company was the South Staffordshire Railway, which began passenger services from a temporary station at Dudley on 1 May 1850. Passenger services along the 'South Staffs' line continued until 6 July 1964. The second company was the Oxford, Worcester & Wolverhampton Railway (OWW), which began its passenger services from Stourbridge to Dudley on 20 December 1852 and through to Wolverhampton on 1 July 1854. This company was taken over by the Great Western Railway (GWR). Services between Stourbridge and Wolverhampton were withdrawn on 30 July 1962. There was also a line from Old Hill to Dudley, which opened on 1 March 1878, whose passenger services last ran on 15 June 1964. In January 1967 the site of Dudley station was remodelled into a Freightliner Terminal, which opened on 16 July 1967. 20 years and a recession later, falling freight business could not justify keeping this open; it closed on 28 September 1986.

Dudley was served by five steam tramway lines. These were the lines to:

Wolverhampton, *which ran from 7 May 1883 to 1899*

Ocker Hill *via Tipton, from 21 January 1884 to 15 June 1904*

Stourbridge, *from 31 May 1884 to 1899*

Birmingham, *via Oldbury and Smethwick, from 30 August 1885 to 1904*

Birmingham, *via Great Bridge and West Bromwich, from 12 October 1885 to 1902.*

It was also served by seven electric tramway lines, to:

Stourbridge, *from 26 July 1899 to 1 March 1930*

Cradley Heath, *from 19 October 1900 to 31 December 1929*

Kingswinford, *from 17 December 1900 to 31 December 1925*

Wolverhampton, *from 13 November 1902 to 1926*

Ocker Hill *via Tipton, from 22 October 1907 to 1 March 1930*

Birmingham, *via Oldbury and Smethwick, from 24 November 1904 to 1 October 1939*

Birmingham, *via Great Bridge and West Bromwich, from 30 May 1902 to 1 October 1939.*

Dudley was served by one trolleybus route operated by Wolverhampton Corporation. This opened on 8 July 1927. Its terminus was in Stone Street, just off Priory Road, on a cobbled area also used as the site of the town's fish market and public weighbridge. Here the trolleybuses made a very tortuous circle, turning sharply in front of the Saracen's Head to enter the terminus in Stone Street. It became Wolverhampton's last trolleybus route and closed on 5 March 1967. Motor omnibus services began in direct competition to tramways c1924, run by a variety of companies. Formal agreement over the replacement of tramway services on 10 September 1929 saw these operated by the Birmingham & Midland Motor Omnibus Co Ltd, or Midland Red, who came to dominate bus services in the town. At their peak they operated 47 routes from the bus station in Porter's Field. All Midland Red services were taken over by the West Midlands Transport Executive on 1 October 1969 and bus services are now provided by their successor, Travel West Midlands, amongst others.

Dudley Station c1950 ZZZ05289 (Dudley Libraries)

Local Government

Dudley's growth was fostered by the Dudley Town Act 1791 under which it was governed by Town Commissioners, who held their first meeting on 5 July 1791. They could levy a rate to fund many of the improvements needed at that time, and could also appoint officers to superintend these improvements. In the 19th century Dudley benefited from various pieces of national legislation. The Reform Act, passed on 5 June 1832, reinstated the town's right to return MPs; the first to be elected was Sir John Campbell. Two years later, the Poor Law of 1834 established a system of parish unions. Under this a Dudley Union was formed in 1836, comprising the parishes of Dudley, Sedgley, Tipton, Rowley Regis and Dudley Castle Hill, covering 18,040 acres and 134,125 people. The Union was badly run from the outset, for its Board of Guardians was inefficient. Matters were eventually sorted out in the 1850s. A new workhouse was built at Shaver's End, which opened in April 1859 and later formed the kernel of the former Burton Road Hospital.

The Board of Guardians were not the only ineffectual public officers - the Town Commissioners ran them a close second. Their record on health was especially poor, and in 1852 the Dudley Board of Health replaced them. Persistent local pressure resulted in the passing of a Charter of Incorporation for Dudley on 3 April 1865. Under this instrument the borough was divided into seven wards: St Thomas's, Castle, St Edmund's, St James's, St John's, Netherton, and Woodside.

In 1868 the Boundary Act extended the boundaries of the Parliamentary Borough of Dudley to incorporate the Municipal Borough of Dudley, plus the extra-parochial grounds of Dudley Castle Hill and the parishes of Quarry Bank and Brierley Hill and the districts of Pensnett and Brockmoor and of Old Hill and Cradley Heath.

In 1888, under the provisions of the Local Government Act, Dudley was declared to be a county borough, and in 1928 a local Act of Parliament enlarged the borough to include the Castle and Castle and Priory wards, formerly in Staffordshire. The West Midlands Order of 1965 further increased the County Borough of Dudley to include Brierley Hill, Coseley and Sedgley UDCs, with effect from 1 April 1966; and the Local Government Act of 1973 created the present Dudley Metropolitan Borough Council with the addition of the former boroughs of Halesowen and Stourbridge on 1 April 1974.

Sequence of Photographs

Most of the photographs in this book were taken between the late 1940s and 1970. They form an evocative record of the town, taken at a time when it was undergoing a transformation from its 18th and 19th century form into that seen in the late 20th century. Familiar landmarks were disappearing and new ones emerging. The photographs have been arranged as a gentle perambulation around Dudley, and each subsequent image is never too far away from the previous one. Enjoy the walk.

CENTRAL
DUDLEY

The Parish Church c1955 D103050a

Its official name is the Church of St James, but everyone in Dudley knows it as 'top church.' This reflects its prominent position on the crown of a hill and at the junction of Upper High Street and High Street. Erected in 1817 to designs by William Brookes of London, the Bath stone building cost a staggering £24,000. The tip of the spire reaches 175ft above the ground. Top church has been restored on a number of occasions. During the most recent of these it was discovered that the building has an iron frame - most unusual for churches, but not too surprising for an area surrounded by ironworks.

High Street, The Seven Stars 1955 ZZZ05274 (A W Foster/Dudley Photographic Society/Dudley Archives)

Much of Dudley town centre has been redeveloped since 1960, sweeping away many buildings of great character, such as the Seven Stars Inn, which stood at 20-21 High Street. On the day that it was photographed, rain was drying on the road and pavement as someone retreated to enjoy the comforts inside. Ansells Brewery was founded in Aston, Birmingham in 1857, and once had numerous tied houses in the Black Country before the company became a subsidiary of Allied Breweries Ltd.

High Street and the Parish Church c1955 D103036

Dudley High Street is quite short compared to those in neighbouring towns. This view up towards top church takes in about half of it. The prominence of the church tower is emphasised well. Many of the shops on the left remain, whilst most of those on the right were demolished in the early 1970s for the building of the Trident Shopping Centre. Immediately next to top church on the left is the Co-op Emporium, and facing each other across the street are departments of F W Cook Ltd, who were drapers, china and glass dealers, and house furnishers.

Market Place, Old Town Hall 1860 ZZZ05276 (Author's Collection)

This is amongst the earliest photographs taken of Dudley. The Old Town Hall was demolished to make way for the fountain, which still stands there. When erected c1660, the building boasted many 'modern' facilities, including a whipping-post, stocks, and a pillory 'for the correction of malefactors.' In later years it was used as a police station and magistrates' court. The posters on the front proclaim the annual Castle Fete. Market stalls can be seen to either side behind the hall. In 1868 it was remarked that the Old Town Hall's 'demolition was generally spoken of regretfully, and the quaint old structure regarded with the kindest feelings.'

Market Place, The Dudley Fountain 1868 ZZZ05277 (Author's Collection)

Replacing the Old Town Hall was the Dudley Fountain, presented to the town by the Earl of Dudley. The drinking fountain was dedicated to the townspeople by Georgina, Countess of Dudley, on 17 October 1867. It was the work of the London sculptor Mr Forsyth and cost £3,000. The figures on top represent 'Industry in General' and 'Industry in Particular.' Water flowed from the mouths of the dolphins on each side to fill drinking troughs for cattle and horses, whilst drinking cups, which were filled from the lions' mouths on each side, catered for human thirst.

▶ *The Criterion Cinema,*
The Interior 1958
ZZZ05278 (Dudley Archives)

The Criterion Electric Theatre opened on 27 February 1911 in modest premises to the rear of Market Place. These were redeveloped from the autumn of 1922 onwards to form a modern cinema with a prominent crush hall entrance on Market Place. This opened on 17 November 1923, and on 11 November 1929 the cinema reopened fully equipped to screen talking pictures. Once one of eight cinemas in Dudley, the Criterion closed on 29 September 1956. The auditorium was stripped its seats and used as a warehouse by Broadmead, a local chain of electrical dealers - a television, then cinema's deadly rival, can be seen at the rear!

▶ *Market Place, Looking West c1955*
D103029

The Criterion Cinema, just off camera to the right, was still open when this view was taken. This is the heart of the town, and markets have been held here for 800 years; the basic size and shape of the market place has remained largely the same throughout that period, as evinced by map evidence. The shops represented here are a mix of chain multiples (Burtons, Boots, Timpsons shoes, Woolworth's and the Maypole Dairy Co), and local chains, such as Alfred Preedy & Sons (second from right), who were tobacconists, with other shops in the Fountain Arcade and Hall Street. Until 1930 the area in front of the fountain had been the tram terminus, and one traction pole from the tramway overhead can be see on the extreme right.

▼ *detail from* ZZZ05278

▶ *Market Place, Looking East c1955*
D103028

Not too many of the Dudley Fountain's drinking cups seem to have survived the almost 90 years since it was dedicated to the town, and it is doubtful that all that many horses and cattle still drank from the troughs, whose rims seem now to provide convenient seating. Is that some tram track peering through the tarmac bottom left? - quite possibly. In the distance, on the extreme right, the tower of St Edmund's Church can be glimpsed. Most of the buildings we see here have been replaced, but because their replacements have followed the same building line, the impression of change is less than is realised until evidence such as this is seen.

Market Day 1957 ZZZ05279
(Dudley Photographic Society/Dudley
Archives)

Winter sun lights up the hustle and
bustle of market day. This view, probably
from the upper storey of Woolworth's,
reveals otherwise hidden details of the
Dudley Fountain, including the figures
of industry and the upper troughs
fed by marine horses. 'Tannoy'-style
speakers have also been fitted. A traffic
policeman controlling the pedestrian
crossing has halted a Midland Red bus.
So strong is the sun that it is casting a
reflection of the Midland Bank's address
onto the road surface: '226 Market Place.'

The Steps to the Gentlemen's Public Conveniences, Market Place 1958 ZZZ05281 (Ivan S/Dudley Photographic Society/ Dudley Archives)

There is innocence about this image which says a lot about the way times and attitudes have changed over the last 50 years or so. Imagine trying to take a photograph in a gent's toilet today! Imagine finding one that wasn't vandalised, or even one that was open at all! These toilets were at the Hall and New Street end of Market Place, where their modern replacements still stand. The care that went into the use of glazed brick, and the decorative wrought ironwork in the railings and gate, is remarkable.

Market Place at Night 1958 ZZZ05280 (F Rogers/ Dudley Photographic Society/Dudley Archives)

Not a single soul can be seen in this dramatic view of the Market Place at night. The Market Place is now pedestrianised, but a one-way traffic system was long used through it in an attempt to ease traffic congestion – sad to say, it was rarely this quiet!

The Sculptured Frieze, Birdcage Walk c1965 D103123

The regeneration of the south side of Dudley town centre began in 1962. First to be completed was a pedestrian way linking Castle Street with the bus station. This was called Birdcage Walk, and once included an aviary housing tropical birds. It also features a sculptured frieze by the artist Bainbridge Copnall, which was made from fibreglass and powdered aluminium. It measures 25ft by 7ft and depicts, at each end, chain making and coal mining, with a mother and child in the centre representing education.

A Newsvendor at the Corner of Hall Street 1957 ZZZ05282 (Graham Know/Dudley Photographic Society/Dudley Archives)

This newsvendor's pitch is at the junction of Hall Street with Market Place. Montague Burton – 'The Tailor of Taste' – provides a stylish backdrop to the scene. Burton's were astute in business. They sold suits and other tailoring that could be paid for in instalments. Many of their shops also had billiard or snooker halls above, the idea being that men coming to use these facilities would be attracted into the shop beneath. Their stores had striking architecture, often with Egyptian influences, and each had two foundation stones laid by members of the family.

*Castle Street and
St Edmund's Church c1955*
D103026

Much that can be seen to
the left and right in this
photograph was swept away
in redevelopment during the
1960s, with the exception of
St Edmund's Church and the
buildings adjoining it. The
view is from the end of the
Market Place, with New Street
to the left and Fisher Street
to the right. Several tramway
traction poles can be seen,
one prominently to the left
of a sign that optimistically
offers a ticket and parcels
agency service to the Great
Western Railway seven years
after it was nationalised
(left). A church dedicated
to St Edmund has stood on
this site since at least the
12th century; indeed, it is
mentioned in a Papal Bull
by Pope Lucius III dated
1182. The original church
was demolished in 1646
during the Civil War, and its
replacement was not built
until 1724.

Tower Street, Looking North c1890
ZZZ05283 (Author's Collection)

Despite the leaves on the trees, many chimneys are smoking along Tower Street. It is clearly a hot day, as most of the windows are open! There also appears to be some form of fence or gate across the end of the road. Tower Street was the subject of redevelopment in the late 1930s, when most of the buildings on the left here were replaced by a police and fire station complex which opened in 1940.

Tower Street, Looking South 1959 ZZZ05284
(W J Clift/Dudley Photographic Society/Dudley Archives)

However, by 1959, demolition was not a fate that had befallen all of the buildings seen on the right of Tower Street in photograph ZZZ05283 (page 30); clearly, those in the centre foreground here are the same ones that we see in the earlier photograph - the gas lamp standard is even still there! A mother and son are just passing the offices of Thomas Woodhouse & Sons, who were a local firm of bakers.

The Civic Gardens and the Castle Keep c1955 D103039

For a very built-up area, Dudley has always had a number of green, open spaces, including the Civic Gardens, situated between Priory Road and The Broadway, opposite the Council House. The facilities are spartan, but a few generations have found some respite here, especially during lunchtime, with a walk or rest in this pleasant spot, which was laid out as part of the Council House scheme completed in December 1935.

31

▲ *The Ruins, Priory Park c1955* D103041

The Cluniac priory of St James stood about ¼ mile west of Dudley Castle. Gervase Pagnell built it in 1161, and the priory prospered until the reign of Henry VIII, when, along with many others, it was dissolved. 30 years after its dissolution, a visitor observed that it was a great pity 'to see both the church and the monuments defaced as they were.' By 1776 a tanner had set up his business in the ruins, and so had a thread maker, and by 1801, these had been joined by a glass engraver and a fire iron polisher.

▶ *Priory Park c1955* D103043

Eventually the Earl of Dudley gave the priory ruins to the people of Dudley, and the council laid out the grounds to form a public park, where people can still sit in contemplation, much as their Cluniac forebears did many centuries earlier. Today, perhaps, there are just a few more distractions, such as the young ladies who seem to have caught the eye of the man on the bench here!

*The Rose Garden,
Priory Park c1955*
D103048

Parts of Priory Park were laid out more formally, such as the rose garden. Through the trees in the background can be glimpsed part of the Dudley & Staffordshire Technical College, which, despite recent name changes, is still known to many in the area as 'Dudley Tech.' It was built at a cost of £112,000 between 1933 and 1935, and has been expanded greatly since, both in its size and in the scope of its curriculum.

Castle Street and St Edmund's Church 1968 D103192

After a little wander down to the priory ruins, our perambulation of Dudley has returned to Castle Street, some 13 years on from view D103026 (page 28). The redevelopment referred to there has taken place, and is most evident to the left, where the then new block of shops included a Fine Fare supermarket, once a prominent chain locally. Almost off camera on the right is Stantons music store - a place of wonderment for many in their youth. Their origins were in the business of James Stanton, a pianoforte dealer, but by the 1960s they sold musical instruments and sheet music. Some days, if you were lucky, the likes of Noddy Holder, and other local musical heroes, could be spied in there!

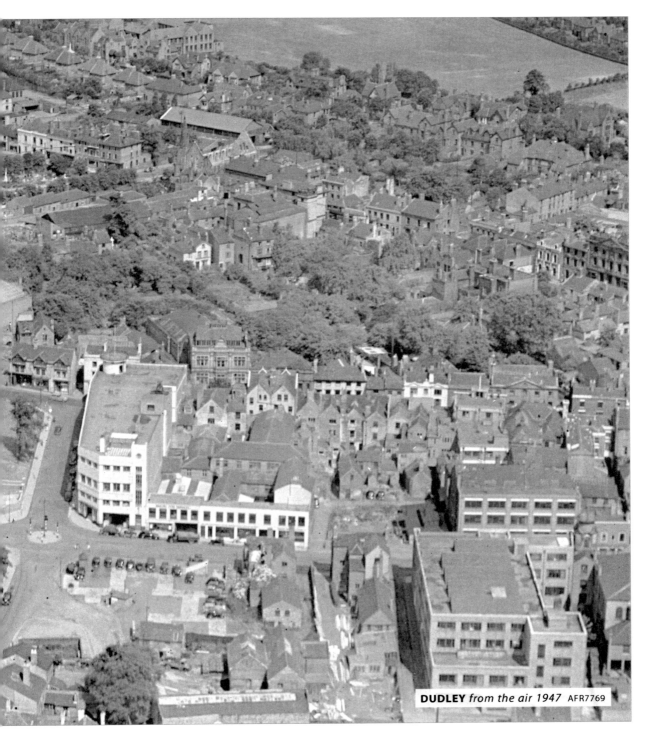

DUDLEY *from the air 1947* AFR7769

Dudley Castle and Entrance from the Air c1930
ZZZ05285 (Author's Collection)

The area surrounding Dudley Castle and Dudley Zoo was originally known as the Conigree. In 1817 a circuitous drive was formed round the hill, and walks were laid out traversing the grounds in different directions. This was the entrance to the castle before it was incorporated into the zoo complex in 1937. The 'air' that the photograph was taken from was probably the tower of St Edmund's Church!

The Gateway to Dudley Castle 1949
D103004

Following the incorporation of the castle into the zoo, its former entrance was used by the Zoological Society for access to their offices and to the Fellows Club, the white building to the left. The statue is of William, Earl of Dudley, and was erected in 1888 'in grateful remembrance of the many benefits conferred by him upon this town.'

Dudley Castle c1950 D103007

A castle at Dudley is first mentioned following the arrival of 'a great and powerful prince of the Kingdom of Mercia' called Dudd, Dodo or Dudo c700. It is said that he 'raised a strong fortress here, which remained until the Conquest.' The keep, seen here above one of the later zoo enclosures, is believed to be the oldest substantive part of the castle, with the exception of fragments of walling in the gatehouse, which can be seen to the right.

▶ *The Castle Keep*
c1960 D103084

We view the keep through the postern gate to the northern end of the castle site. Inside the bailey the keep appears much more complete than it actually is. It was built in this form over a protracted period spanning the late 13th and early 14th centuries, owing to the fluctuating fortunes of the de Somery family who owned it at that time. Here it is seen set against grounds laid out by the Zoological Society in the later 1930s.

◀ *The Castle Keep*
c1955 D103019

Historically, castle baileys were home to many people, and something of that feel is captured in this view of relaxing zoo visitors enjoying sun and ice creams in the mid 1950s. The windowed building in the centre was lodgings added to the castle around 1690, some of the last new construction on the site. Next to that is the rear of the gatehouse, which is contemporary to the keep.

▲ *The View from the Castle Keep c1955* D103054

Almost no building work was carried out at Dudley Castle for the 200 years between 1340 and 1540, but in 1540 John Dudley, later Duke of Northumberland, set about rebuilding the residential block on a grand scale. The results are seen here. From the extreme left are a pantry, kitchen, serving place, buttery, hall, and great chamber, most of which had bedrooms above. In zoo days the single-storey building on the right was the aquarium.

◄ *The Castle Ruins c1955*
D103011

A close up view of John Dudley's handiwork, showing the hall, centre left, and great chamber, centre right. The castle's downfall was in two stages. After the end of the Civil War, it was slighted (or de-fortified). This destroyed the castle walls, turrets and gatehouse, but left the residential side unharmed. The second stage was a major fire on 24 July 1750, which blazed for two days and finished the castle as a residence. Here visitors to the zoo loll about, largely unaware of the history that surrounds them.

The Panoramic View from the Castle Keep c1955
D103016

The one thing that has not changed about Dudley Castle is the spectacular views afforded from Castle Hill. On the apocryphal 'clear day' it is possible to see the Malvern Hills, Bromsgrove, the Lickey Hills, Frankley Beeches, Clent, Abberley and the Clee Hills. Here the view is out over some of the castle's outer buildings along Castle Street and into the Market Place. St Edmund's Church is prominent in the foreground, whilst on the horizon is the outline of St Andrew's Church, Netherton, which is almost as prominent a local landmark as the castle keep itself.

▼ *The Panoramic View from the Castle Keep c1955* D103015

Top church dominates the skyline in this second view from the castle keep. The direction is south-east, and municipal buildings occupy the centre ground. Centre left is the combined police and fire station in Tower Street, referred to earlier. Note the six-storey tower. To the right of this is the Council House, which was opened formally by HRH The Duke of Kent in December 1935. The Civic Gardens lie in front of them.

▶ *The View from the Castle Keep c1955* D103059x

This final view from the castle keep looks due south across the bus station in Porter's Field. Trindle Road runs across the centre of the picture, whilst the corner of Hall Street can be seen centre right. A mixture of Midland Red and Birmingham Corporation buses circle the bus station, whilst the National Projectile Factory dominates the skyline. This massive works was erected in 1915 for the production of artillery shells in the build-up to the big push on the Somme in 1916. After the war it was sold to the Co-operative Wholesale Society, who used it to manufacture hollowware, mainly buckets!

◄ *The Bus Station,
Porter's Field 1960*
ZZZ05286 (W H Massey/
Dudley Photographic
Society/Dudley Archives)

Dudley's bus station
used to be all concrete:
concrete standing,
concrete shelters,
concrete lampposts.
Here the view looks
along Fisher Street
toward Castle Street.
The white buildings
beyond the single-decker
can be seen in the centre
of D103059x (on page
42). The bus itself is on
route D10 to Lodge Farm
Estate via Netherton,
whilst the double-
decker is on route
140 - Birmingham via
Blackheath and Quinton.
A West Bromwich
Corporation bus is
silhouetted against what
is probably the steel
framework for Stantons
in the course of erection.

► *The Entrance to Dudley Zoo,
Castle Hill c1965* D103122

The Dudley Zoological Society was
founded in 1935 to develop a zoo in
the environs of Dudley Castle, and
the Russian-born architect Berthold
Lubetkin (1901-1990) was engaged
to design the buildings and
enclosures. Lubetkin headed the
Tecton architectural practice, and as
a result the 13 reinforced concrete
structures he designed for Dudley
have become known as the Tecton
Buildings. These are Lubetkin's
stylish entrance turnstiles, which
were much admired on the opening
day - 6 May 1937 - as 200,000 of
the 250,000 people who turned up
were refused admission on grounds
of public safety!

The Original Dudley Zoo? 1936 ZZZ05287 (Frank Power/Dudley Archives)

Did Dudley Zoo have a rival? Hardly - this is probably a publicity stunt around the time that the zoo was due to open. Ernest Appleton was a bird dealer in King Street, near to Porter's Field. He was photographed outside his shop with a bird on top of its cage, and two monkeys, one on his shoulder and one in his right hand. Its unlikely that the zoo's directors were troubled by this all that much - 'oo'd go there', for one thing!

The Entrance to Dudley Zoo, Castle Hill c1960 D103067

This view of Berthold Lubetkin's entrance to Dudley Zoo also shows the large letters 'Z', 'O', and 'O', which left little doubt as to what lay beyond. The zoo's managers were very clever in their use of this symbolism, and for many years traded on the slogan: 'Ooz going to Dudley Zoo?' The easel board in front updated visitors about any day-to-day changes in the zoo's operation, and any special events.

Elephants at Dudley Zoo c1965 D103255

The laying out of Dudley Zoo took account of the nature of Castle Hill, and most of the animal enclosures were fitted into the natural or previously formed features. One result of this was the terracing that is so much a feature of the zoo - requiring much climbing by visitors! The terracing is very evident here in this view of some of the elephants.

Lions at Dudley Zoo
c1965 D103156

The Lion Enclosure was one of those specifically accommodated into a natural feature of Castle Hill. Here two of its occupants sun themselves. Today Dudley Zoo, and zoos in general, have moved away from keeping large or exotic animals, which can be seen more in wildlife parks such as the West Midlands Safari Park near Bewdley.

A Gorilla at Dudley Zoo c1965 D103147

The stylish design of Berthold Lubetkin's enclosures at Dudley Zoo is seen to good effect in this view of the Gorilla House. How sad it is that these did not prove to be good buildings in any sense: they did not suit the animals, and they have proven to be difficult and expensive to maintain. Nonetheless, the 13 remaining Lubetkin-designed structures on the zoo site now all enjoy listed building status.

▲ *Castle Hill, The Junction with Tipton Road c1960* D103076

We are looking from just inside Birmingham Road up Castle Hill, with Tipton Road off to the right. On the extreme left is the Station Garage, then an Austin dealership. Behind that is the Station Hotel, a replacement of an earlier building of the same name built in 1936. Between the two buildings runs the railway, at a much lower level. On the opposite side of the road stands the Plaza cinema with the Hippodrome theatre next to it. The Plaza replaced an earlier cinema on the same site, and opened on 28 May 1936. It survived to be Dudley's last cinema.

HIPPODROME
DUDLEY
ENGLAND'S MOST MODERN VARIETY THEATRE
FREE CAR PARK.   'PHONE 201811
NOTE THE NEW TIMES :
TWICE DAILY AT 4 p.m. and 6.30 p.m.
FOR A SHORT SEASON
COMMENCING BOXING DAY
BABES IN THE WOOD
LEN CLIFFORD
GEORGE HIRSTE
HARRY ORCHID AND PARTNER
BARBARA WOOD
THE SEVEN ELLIOTTS
THE CYGNE FOUR
AND FULL COMPANY OF 60 ARTISTS
Usual Prices.   Special Terms for Parties.

◄ *Dudley Hippodrome Advertisement c1938*
ZZZ05288 (Author's Collection)

Dudley Hippodrome replaced the Opera House, which had stood on Castle Hill since 1899 but had been destroyed by fire in November 1936. Built in Art Deco style, the Hippodrome was one of the top ten variety venues in the country. It was part of the premier Moss Empires circuit of theatres, and anybody who was or became anybody in entertainment played there at one time or another. It closed in 1958, but opened briefly as a venue for nude reviews and blue comic shows, closing finally as a theatre in 1964. Since then it has enjoyed life as a bingo hall. This advertisement is for one of the first pantomimes in the new theatre.

49

Dudley Station c1950
ZZZ05289 (Dudley Libraries)

Also at the foot of Castle Hill, on the same side as Dudley Hippodrome, was the railway station, seen here from Castle Hill Road Bridge. Closest to the camera is Dudley South signal box, which projected out from the end of the platform. By this time its lower half had been strengthened with a formidable brick skirt. A pannier tank rests in No 3 bay platform on the ex-GWR side, whilst the ex-LMS platform to the right is alive with passengers.

A Local Train at Dudley Station c1938
ZZZ05290 (Ron Moss)

Trains to Old Hill used No 3 Bay platform at Dudley Station, next to Dudley South Signal Box. There, on 28 December 1963, ex-GWR panniertank locomotive No 6424 and its single coach eject steam from a connecting pipe as they wait their return to Old Hill. The station closed just over 6 months later, on 6 July 1964.

A Tram to Stourbridge 1929
ZZZ05291 (Author's Collection)

Between 26 July 1899 and
1 March 1930 a service of
electric trams ran between the
foot of Castle Hill in Dudley and
Stourbridge, going through
Brierley Hill. For the last ten years
of its working life single-deck
cars like this one, which was
built locally in Tividale in 1919,
worked the tramway. The Tipton
Road junction can be seen in
the background. The tram looks
pretty full - perhaps that is why
all the windows are open!

▶ *A Trolleybus Overhead in Wolverhampton Street 1958* ZZZ05295 (Thera Leighton/Dudley Photographic Society/Dudley Archives)

A Wolverhampton trolleybus is moving from Salop Street in to Wolverhampton Street, and is shortly to pass the quaintly named Ye Old Struggling Man Inn at No 95. This was the last trolleybus route to be operated by Wolverhampton Corporation, and it closed on 5 March 1967. Compared to the same location in recent years, the lack of traffic in this scene is remarkable.

◀ *The Trolleybus Terminus, Stone Street 1955* ZZZ05293 (Dudley Photographic Society/ Dudley Archives)

From 8 July 1927 Dudley was reached by a trolleybus service operated by Wolverhampton Corporation. Its terminus was here in Stone Street, just off Priory Road, on a cobbled area also used as the site of the town's fish market, and where the public weighbridge (left) was relocated from the Market Place in 1904. Behind is the rear entrance to the Fountain Arcade, which was built in 1925. Immediately behind the trolleybus No 650 is part of Dudley's original fire station.

▲ *The Trolleybus Overhead in Wolverhampton Street 1958* ZZZ05294
(Thera Leighton/Dudley Photographic Society/Dudley Archives)

This photograph was taken in Wolverhampton Street, from the corner of Chapel Street, looking towards the town centre. The narrowness of the road meant that the trolleybus overhead had to be quite close together, but at least it could be mounted on a single side arm. North Worcestershire Garages (right) were a local chain specialising in Vauxhall cars and Bedford vans. They also had premises in Stourbridge.

◄ *The Tram Depot on Castle Hill c1903* ZZZ05292
(R S Carpenter Collection)

A view across Dudley Station from the GWR platform, with locomotive 0-6-0ST 1513 coupled to a wagon belonging to M & W Grazebrook Ltd, whose collieries and furnaces were at Parkhead in Netherton. An LNWR coach can be seen to the right. Above is the best photograph known of the Dudley, Stourbridge & District Electric Tramways depot at the foot of Castle Hill. This had two roads inside and one down the outside, on which two trams can be seen parked.

THE CLEARANCE
AREA

Over seven years, between 1962 and 1969, the south side of Dudley town centre was comprehensively redeveloped under what was called the 'Clearance Area' scheme. This took in most of the buildings and streets south of King Street. The scheme was in three phases:

1: Birdcage Walk, associated shops and car park - completed 1964

2: Hall Street redevelopment - completed August 1967

3: Flood Street car park and Churchill Precinct - completed 1969.

From the late 1950s onwards Dudley Council part-funded Dudley Photographic Society to record the Clearance Area ahead of the scheme's commencement. This far-sightedness on their part has left a special record of a vanished part of Dudley.

An Overview of the Clearance Area c1958 ZZZ05296 (Dudley Archives)

From on top of the larger of the two gasholders in the gas works in Bath Street, the view is looking north-west towards the National Projectile Factory on the skyline. Bath Street runs diagonally across the picture, with Vicar Street running off it to the left. The majority of what can be seen in this photograph was due to be demolished within the next five years.

King Street, The Salvation Army Citadel 1958 ZZZ05297 (W J Clift/Dudley Photographic Society/Dudley Archives)

One of the buildings affected by the Clearance Area Scheme was the Salvation Army Citadel in King Street, a stylish interwar building seen in use here. Following the citadel's closure, the Salvation Army found new premises in the town in North Street.

The South Side of King Street 1958
ZZZ05298 (Dudley Photographic Society/Dudley Archives)

A view of the south side of King Street, from Flood Street (right) to Oakeywell Street (left). This was the northern edge of the Clearance Area, and all of the buildings in this view would be consumed by it. The Green Dragon Inn at 20 King Street was unusual in this area in that it was a Joule's house - Joules was a brewer from Stone in Staffordshire, established in 1780.

King Street, South Side 1958 ZZZ05299 (Dudley Photographic Society/Dudley Archives)

A view of the south side of King Street, looking the other way from ZZZ05298 (above), from Oakeywell Street (left) to Flood Street (right). This is now the edge of the Flood Street car park, and the site of a pedestrian footbridge linking this to the Churchill Precinct. James Parkes & Son (left) were cycle dealers and repairers at No 7 King Street.

Trindle Road, From Claughton Road 1960 ZZZ05300 (W H Massey/Dudley Photographic Society/Dudley Archives)

Trindle Road was never like this! Until the opening of the Dudley Southern By-Pass it was a notorious bottleneck, but here it is unpopulated save for one man and two Ford Anglias. All of the buildings in this view have gone. John Douglas & Sons Ltd, behind the man crossing the road, were legging manufacturers - their telegram address was 'Sportsman.'

61

▶ *Porter Street,
Looking from
Trindle Road 1958*
ZZZ05301 (W J Clift/
Dudley Photographic
Society/Dudley Archives)

Porter Street led into
Terry Street, which
can be seen beyond.
Isaiah Woodhall &
Sons Ltd (right) were
hearth furniture
makers - little
brushes and shovels
for making up and
tending coal fires.
Their manufacture
was something of
a Dudley specialty,
and had evolved
out of bedstead and
fender manufacture,
most of which was
concentrated around
Wellington Road.

◀ *Dudley Row 1958*
ZZZ05302 (Dudley
Photographic Society/
Dudley Archives)

With so many properties
to be compulsorily
purchased, there was an
enquiry held, ahead of
which all of the premises
affected were inspected.
Here, little to the
amusement of the lady
in the washhouse,
J McD Fairweather (left)
and W Parker (right)
get lost in their work
- whereas she clearly
wishes them just to get
lost!

▲ *detail of* ZZZ05301 (W J Clift/Dudley
Photographic Society/Dudley Archives)

◀ *From Oakeywell Street, Looking
towards Hall Street 1959* ZZZ05303
(C N F Lewis/Dudley Photographic Society/
Dudley Archives)

An amazing jumble of buildings,
amassed over a number of years, stood
behind these properties in Hall Street.
The clue as to the location comes
from the partial shop front visible on the
right. This is W Baker & Sons, boot dealers
of 33 Hall Street.

*◄ Oakeywell Street,
The National Projectile
Works 1958* ZZZ05305
(Dudley Photographic Society/
Dudley Archives)

40 years had passed since
this works last produced an
artillery shell, and, as noted
on page 42, it had become
a central manufactory
of hollowware for the
Co-operative Wholesale
Society nationally. This led
to its local nickname of
'the bucket works', because
buckets, especially buckets
for mops, were made there.
The water tower used to
be adorned with the
letters 'CWS.'

The Rear of 25 Campbell Street 1958
ZZZ05306 (Dudley Photographic Society/Dudley Archives)

Campbell Street linked Oakeywell Street with Bond Street, and No 25 was typical of much of the housing in it. There is a slightly posed air about this photograph: all parties stare at the camera, including a shadowy figure in the doorway. The horseshoe above the door just about sums this up - Campbell Street's luck had run out.

▲ *Oakeywell Street, Looking towards the Gas Works 1958* ZZZ05304
(Dudley Photographic Society/Dudley Archives)

This part of Oakeywell Street at least seemed to be pretty much abandoned to its fate, and there does not seem to be much left of Bond Street or John Street to obstruct a clear view of the towering gas works beyond. Left of a curiously tall and oddly bent telegraph pole is a gas lamp standard.

◀ *Bond Street 1958* ZZZ05307
(Dudley Photographic Society/Dudley Archives)

Almost all of Bond Street can be seen in this view, which looks towards King Street. The row of buildings from left to centre had clearly all been shops at one time or another, and one retains its Typhoo Tea advertisements on the windows. Perhaps above all of the other photographs in this record, this one emphasises the density of the old buildings shortly to be cleared.

The Rear of 34-36 Bond Street 1958 ZZZ05308
(Dudley Photographic Society/
Dudley Archives)

For all its closeness and primitive facilities, this courtyard to the rear of houses in Bond Street looks very clean. Carpets, rugs and mats are piled up on the left, awaiting or just having undergone a beating, and the gutter to the right is running with soapy water. The little girl is clean and well dressed, and, above all else - safe!

Looking towards Bond Street 1958
ZZZ05309 (Dudley Photographic Society/
Dudley Archives)

Four children in their Sunday best cross
in front of the camera, which is pointed
towards Bond Street - in all probability
they are going to Sunday School. The
prominent buildings, centre left, were
the premises of William Nayler Ltd, who
were iron merchants in Bond Street.
There is an impressive amount of
timber shoring up the left-hand side of
the building!

69

Flood Street, From New Mill Street 1958 ZZZ05310 (Dudley Photographic Society/Dudley Archives)

A view of 57 to 59 Flood Street, the former being the Good Fellows Arms Inn, and the latter Broome's shop, who were agents for the Birmingham-made Hercules bicycles. The way that the initial has been painted out in front of the surname suggests that Horace Broome, who was a wireless accessories dealer at the same address in 1940, is not running this shop anymore. The impressive gas lamp is one of the sewer-venting kind, and the way that the lamp has been placed straddling the wall of the gents behind is clever.

Bath Street, Looking South 1958 ZZZ05311 (Dudley Photographic Society/Dudley Archives)

This is Bath Street at the intersection of Church Street. The Blue Gates Inn (left) is No 58 Church Street, and the road carries on past the gas lamp on the right. The pub was tied to Edwin Holden's Hopden Brewery, situated in George Street, Woodsetton, and seems to have at least one customer. Ahead and right is Martins Hill Street.

Church Street 1958 ZZZ05312 (Dudley Photographic Society/Dudley Archives)

E C Lewis had built this impressive-looking warehouse for his tea and provisions business in 1898, but exactly 60 years later it was not looking its best. This was clearly not a shop, as we can see from the two deep taking-in doors on the ground and first floors. The lower one would have been for loading directly onto handcarts, and the upper one for raising or lowering goods off or to the bed of a cart.

Fountain Street, From Spring Gardens 1958
ZZZ05313 (W J Clift/Dudley Photographic Society/Dudley Archives)

Perhaps somebody knows something, or somebody should be told something, because there seems to be new building going on in this view! The pub with its name blanked out stands at the top of Church Street, the portion seen going off to the right in the photograph of Bath Street looking south (ZZZ05311, page 70).

▶ *Red Hill from Spring Gardens 1958*
ZZZ05314 (Dudley Photographic Society/ Dudley Archives)

We are looking up Red Hill towards Prospect Row from Spring Gardens, with the gas works on the right. Red Hill seems aptly named, and forms quite a bank ahead. The road turning left off Red Hill part way up is Tetnall Street, whilst on the horizon to the left more of the National Projectile Works can be seen. Low winter sun gives the entire scene a dramatic look.

◀ *The Rear of 15-17 Prospect Row 1958*
ZZZ05315 (Dudley Photographic Society/ Dudley Archives)

Two ladies look on as a third goes about her work at the rear of houses in Prospect Row. Once again, although 'primitive' by modern standards, the area looks very clean and tidy. The tap on the right replaced a hand-pump which formerly stood there, and the lumpy nature of the water pipe indicates that it is made of lead.

▲ *detail from* ZZZ05315

◄ *Bath Street, at the Junction with Vicar Street 1958* ZZZ05316 (W H Massey/ Dudley Photographic Society/ Dudley Archives)

Here there is quite a contrast in appearance. Perhaps it is because industrial premises are expected to be a bit grimy that the Dudley Brass & Bronze Foundry looks as though it might still be working, whilst the shop next door is - one would hope - closed. The gas works was immediately behind these buildings, and Blowers Green station was just a short distance to the right down New Road.

THE OUTSKIRTS

By the time that most of the photographs in this book were taken, Dudley had become responsible for the administration of quite a large area. The final selection of photographs looks at some of these further flung places.

Kate's Hill, St John's Church c1965 D103115

St John's Church, Kate's Hill was erected in 1840 at a cost of £3,000, four years ahead of the ecclesiastical parish it serves, which was created on 15 October 1844. It was unusual in a number of respects, including the inclusion of ten tubular bells in the tower and for having galleries on three sides (hence the height of the nave), which gave it 730 sittings. A parish hall was added in 1932.

▲ *Netherton, Swan Street, Baptist End*
c1938 ZZZ05317 (Dudley Archives)

We are looking north towards the bend in
Swan Street, with Round Street beyond. On
the bend of the road stands a 'tin chapel',
actually Baptist End People's Mission Hall,
which appears to have been extended
slightly to the rear. In the foreground the
ground is undeveloped, and clay and ash
show through.

◄ *detail from* ZZZ05317

Netherton, Six Foot Road 1958 ZZZ05318 (Dudley Photographic Society/Dudley Archives)

If this photograph is to be believed, Six Foot Road, Netherton is aptly named; it was wide enough for these two children to enjoy a walk in the winter sunshine, though.

Woodside, 71-72 High Street 1958 ZZZ05319 (Dudley Photographic Society/Dudley Archives)

Both the Crown Inn in the background, and these two properties, are in High Street, Woodside. A pair of council inspectors pays a call at No 72. The state of the path leading to these houses is very poor, and from their low-lying situation they must have been exceedingly damp.

Woodside, 453 Stourbridge Road 1958 ZZZ05320 (Dudley Photographic Society/Dudley Archives)

Subsidence was much in evidence along Stourbridge Road, Woodside at this time. Here a 'Complete Funeral Director' at No 453 is in danger of toppling over as two people pass with a Christmas tree. Cracks are evident in the next property too. This problem was caused by mining and the general instability of the ground. Elsewhere along Stourbridge Road, some houses just sank, so that their upper storey windows were at ground level!

▲ *Harts Hill, Stourbridge Road,
from Chapel Street 1958* ZZZ05321
(Dudley Photographic Society/Dudley Archives)

Subsidence is again very much in evidence
here further down Stourbridge Road at
Harts Hill - it is entirely responsible for
the higgledy-piggledy way in which the
houses seem to be resting against each
other in this fashion. Although it may
appear to be another electric tramway
traction pole, the one seen in the centre
foreground is in fact a sewer ventilation
pipe.

◄ *detail from* ZZZ05321

▲ *Harts Hill, 46 to 48 Garratt Street 1958*
ZZZ05322 (Dudley Photographic Society/
Dudley Archives)

Garratt Street, Harts Hill, was named after
Alderman Job T Garratt, who was very
influential in securing improvements for
the Woodside and Harts Hill areas in the
late 19th and early 20th centuries. By the
late 1950s the street that bore his name
was a little the worse for wear. However,
the child at No 46 was secure behind
those boards.

▶ *detail from* ZZZ05322

Harts Hill, 91-92 Garratt Street 1958 ZZZ05323 (Dudley Photographic Society/Dudley Archives)

Subsidence is evident in Garratt Street too, both in this photograph and in ZZZ05322 (page 82). Here one of the council inspectors we saw earlier in High Street, Woodside is caught doing a plumb bob test to indicate the degree to which No 92 is leaning over. The doorway behind him appears to be leaning more out of true than his plumb line suggests, which is rather odd!

Harts Hill, Canal Street 1958
ZZZ05324
(Dudley Photographic Society/Dudley Archives)

The waterway which gives this street its name is the Pensnett Canal, which was privately built by the Earl of Dudley to serve his Round Oak Ironworks. It lies to the right of the scene. Again there is some subsidence affecting the houses in the centre, made all the clearer by the near vertical lamppost.

INDEX

FRITH PRODUCTS & SERVICES

Francis Frith would doubtless be pleased to know that the pioneering publishing venture he started in 1860 still continues today. Over a hundred and forty years later, The Francis Frith Collection continues in the same innovative tradition and is now one of the foremost publishers of vintage photographs in the world. Some of the current activities include:

INTERIOR DECORATION

Today Frith's photographs can be seen framed and as giant wall murals in thousands of pubs, restaurants, hotels, banks, retail stores and other public buildings throughout the country. In every case they enhance the unique local atmosphere of the places they depict and provide reminders of gentler days in an increasingly busy and frenetic world.

PRODUCT PROMOTIONS

Frith products are used by many major companies to promote the sales of their own products or to reinforce their own history and heritage. Frith promotions have been used by Hovis bread, Courage beers, Scots Porage Oats, Colman's mustard, Cadbury's foods, Mellow Birds coffee, Dunhill pipe tobacco, Guinness, and Bulmer's Cider.

GENEALOGY AND FAMILY HISTORY

As the interest in family history and roots grows world-wide, more and more people are turning to Frith's photographs of Great Britain for images of the towns, villages and streets where their ancestors lived; and, of course, photographs of the churches and chapels where their ancestors were christened, married and buried are an essential part of every genealogy tree and family album.

FRITH PRODUCTS

All Frith photographs are available Framed or just as Mounted Prints and Posters (size 23 x 16 inches). These may be ordered from the address below. Other products available are - Address Books, Calendars, Jigsaws, Canvas Prints, Postcards and local and prestige books.

THE INTERNET

Already ninety thousand Frith photographs can be viewed and purchased on the internet through the Frith websites and a myriad of partner sites.

For more detailed information on Frith products, look at this site:
www.francisfrith.com

See the complete list of Frith Books at: www.francisfrith.com
This web site is regularly updated with the latest list of publications from The Francis Frith Collection. If you wish to buy books relating to another part of the country that your local bookshop does not stock, you may purchase on-line.

For further information, trade, or author enquiries please contact us at the address below:
The Francis Frith Collection, Unit 6, Oakley Business Park, Wylye Road, Dinton, Wiltshire SP3 5EU.
Tel: +44 (0)1722 716 376 Fax: +44 (0)1722 716 881 Email: sales@francisfrith.co.uk

---

See Frith products on the internet at www.francisfrith.com

FREE PRINT OF YOUR CHOICE

Mounted Print
Overall size 14 x 11 inches (355 x 280mm)

Choose any Frith photograph in this book.
Simply complete the Voucher opposite and
return it with your remittance for £3.50 (to cover
postage and handling) and we will print the
photograph of your choice in SEPIA (size 11 x 8
inches) and supply it in a cream mount with a
burgundy rule line (overall size 14 x 11 inches).
Please note: aerial photographs and
photographs with a reference number
starting with a "Z" are not Frith photographs
and cannot be supplied under this offer.
Offer valid for delivery to one UK address only.

**PLUS: Order additional Mounted Prints
at HALF PRICE - £10.00 each** (normally £20.00)
If you would like to order more Frith prints from
this book, possibly as gifts for friends and family,
you can buy them at half price (with no
additional postage and handling costs).

PLUS: Have your Mounted Prints framed
For an extra £19.00 per print you can have your
mounted print(s) framed in an elegant polished
wood and gilt moulding, overall size
16 x 13 inches (no additional postage and
handling required).

IMPORTANT!

**These special prices are only available if you use
this form to order. You must use the ORIGINAL
VOUCHER on this page (no copies permitted). We
can only despatch to one UK address. This offer
cannot be combined with any other offer.**

Send completed Voucher form to:
**The Francis Frith Collection, Unit 6,
Oakley Business Park, Wylye Road,
Dinton, Wiltshire SP3 5EU**

CHOOSE A PHOTOGRAPH FROM THIS BOOK

Voucher  for **FREE** and Reduced Price Frith Prints

*Please do not photocopy this voucher. Only the original is valid,
so please fill it in, cut it out and return it to us with your order.*

Picture ref no	Page no	Qty	Mounted @ £10.00	Framed + £19.00	Total Cost £
		1	Free of charge*	£	£
			£10.00	£	£
			£10.00	£	£
			£10.00	£	£
			£10.00	£	£
			£10.00	£	£

*Please allow 28 days
for delivery.
Offer available to one
UK address only*

* Post & handling	£3.80
Total Order Cost	£

Title of this book . . . .

I enclose a cheque/postal order for £ . . . .
made payable to 'The Francis Frith Collection'

OR please debit my Mastercard / Visa / Maestro card,
details below

Card Number:

Issue No (Maestro only):   Valid from (Maestro):

Card Security Number: Expires:

Signature:

Name Mr/Mrs/Ms . . . .

Address . . . .

. . . .

. . . .

. . . . Postcode . . . .

Daytime Tel No . . . .

Email . . . .

Valid to 31/12/14

Can you help us with information about any of the Frith photographs in this book?

We are gradually compiling an historical record for each of the photographs in the Frith archive. It is always fascinating to find out the names of the people shown in the pictures, as well as insights into the shops, buildings and other features depicted.

If you recognize anyone in the photographs in this book, or if you have information not already included in the author's caption, do let us know. We would love to hear from you, and will try to publish it in future books or articles.

An Invitation from The Francis Frith Collection to Share Your Memories

The 'Share Your Memories' feature of our website allows members of the public to add personal memories relating to the places featured in our photographs, or comment on others already added. Seeing a place from your past can rekindle forgotten or long held memories. Why not visit the website, find photographs of places you know well and add YOUR story for others to read and enjoy? We would love to hear from you!

www.francisfrith.com/memories

Our production team

Frith books are produced by a small dedicated team at offices near Salisbury. Most have worked with the Frith Collection for many years. All have in common one quality: they have a passion for the Frith Collection.

Frith Books and Gifts

We have a wide range of books and gifts available on our website utilising our photographic archive, many of which can be individually personalised.

www.francisfrith.com